Don't Create an Ishmael, When You Were Promised an Isaac

Don't Create an Ishmael, When You Were Promised an Isaac

"A Journey to the Promise"

(Based on Genesis Chapters 12-21)

By:
Diamond D. McClam

XULON PRESS

Xulon Press
2301 Lucien Way #415
Maitland, FL 32751
407.339.4217
www.xulonpress.com

Printed in the United States of America.

ISBN-13: 978-1-6322-1329-7
Ebook: 978-1-6322-1330-3

Table of Contents

Introduction

There are times in life, that we have made concessions and adjustments to God's perfect will for our lives. This book will discuss the importance of waiting on the promises of God, without making personal pit-stops that could interfere with our destiny. If we are honest, this is an area that people of all ages struggle. The opportunity to fail is so great in the eyes of so many, that we make adjustments that can make the possibility of failing less likely. There have been people who chose their spouse because of convenience and safety. There are people that have chosen their career path out of comfort. We are sometimes in a hurry to move forward and are not willing to wait on God.

This book will take the opportunity to allow you to question yourself regarding your life decisions. My hope and prayer is that this book will change your life forever. My prayer is that you will submit to God's will for your life. Jeremiah 29:11, "For I know the thoughts that I think toward you, saith the Lord, thoughts of peace, and not of evil, to give you an expected end." This book will allow you to see that even Fathers of the Faith have struggled to wait on God. However, you do not have to make decisions that will create dysfunction in your life. The destiny God has in store for you is unique and hand crafted by Him. Please allow God to perfect the masterpiece of your destiny, without your interference.

Chapter 1

The Promise

(Genesis Ch. 12)

Abram receives a promise from God that he would be the Father of Many Nations. Abram is now 75 years old and has no children. He was told by God to leave his family, land, and all that was familiar to him. Abram obeys the word from God and grabs his wife, his nephew Lot, and all they could and went into the land of Canaan. The promise that God gave Abram was not to Lot, but Abram loved him so much that he brought Lot along with him. It seems that Abram was excited about this promise, and he left immediately!

However, he started making a few concessions for what was promised. Abram brought an extra person, lied about his relationship to his wife because of fear, and started on this new journey towards Canaan in his own understanding. We, as people just like Abram, have received and are receiving promises from God right now. We have to be careful not to start making adjustments to God's directives for the promises that God has for us. God allowed a situation in which Abram lied to come together for his good. God protected Abram in such a way that He placed plagues on the house of Pharoah, so that Abram could be together with his wife. God never told Abram to lie about his relationship with his wife, and say that she was his sister, but Abram did so out of fear.

Chapter 2

The Choice

(Genesis Chapter 13)

Abram was blessed by God by the Egyptians. Abram was scared for is life and lied about his relationship with Sarai. God allowed plagues to come upon the Egyptians, which led to them asking Abram about his relation to Sarai. The Egyptians were ready to get them out of the country, Pharaoh even gave them gifts to leave. This was one of the nicest "Get Out" moments in history, because of God. God will allow things to happen so that people will understand what you mean to Him. Abram understood the dire situation that God had just brought him out of, and he went to the altar that he built to worship and call unto the Lord. Abram understood that his blessings came from the Lord.

Abram is now thanking the Lord for covering them and for leading Him. Abram has a choice to make regarding his nephew, Lot. Abram and Lot's staff, or servants, are getting into fights and it was bringing unrest into the trip. I do not recall God telling Abram to take Lot with him. God said, "Get out of your country, from thy family, from thy Father's house unto a land that I will show thee." (Genesis 12:1). However, because of his love for Lot, he took Lot along with Him on this blessed journey. As you are reading this book, please remember this statement and place it in your heart.

Every one cannot go with you where you are going! Every one cannot go with you where you are going! This statement is so important that it is written twice. It is important to know that you can be a blessing to others. You can help them, but they may not be able to be on the road with you. Abram understood that he and Lot had to separate for them to be able to move forward. There are some situations, and people, that you must let go! God may allow them to come back into your life, but for this season, they cannot be involved in your life. Abram allowed Lot to choose his route. Lot saw the green pastures going toward Sodom and Gomorra, and chose that path. Abram showed Godly love for his nephew by letting him choose his path to travel. There are some things that we can see in this instance:

1. We must be careful who we decide to take along with us to our promise.

2. Everyone can't go with you to your promise.

3. A separation may have to take place.

4. Don't be afraid of Divine Separation. (A separation that is ordained by God).

5. Ask God who should go with you, and don't just choose!

God is so gracious that he gives us directions, and still allows us to have free will along the journey. God could easily pick us up and place us in our moment of promise without giving us an opportunity to falter. However, God allows us to walk through different situations to learn new things about Him, others, and ourselves. It is important to notice that Lot took no thought about how his choice would effect Abram or

Sarai. He chose what he thought was best for him. He chose by his own selfish desire of success. In Genesis 12, it does not even say that Lot said "Thank You" to Abram for taking him along this great journey. We must also see that in the midst of it all, God blessed Abram. God blessed Abram for his faithfulness, kindness, love, and faith. After this, God spoke to Abram and told him to look North, South, East, and West, and it would all be his. God also said that He will make his seed as the dust of the Earth. God blessed Abram in his humble state.

Questions

1. Why did God allow Abram to take Lot with him?

2. Why did Abram allow Lot to choose which path to take?

Prayer

Father God in the Name of Jesus, I thank you for the Promise upon my life. I thank you for loving me! Lord, I ask you to give me the strength to accept any divine separation in my life. Please give me the strength to have conversations that need to take place. Lord, I want to be in your will with my connections and along this journey. Please lead and guide me along the way! I love you and I thank you! In Jesus' name. Amen!

Chapter 3

The Rescue

(Genesis Chapter 14)

In the midst of the journey to your promise, there may be some issues that attempt to take you off course. Abram receives word that his nephew, Lot, and his family have been captured. Abram, with the loving heart that he had, knew that he needed to help his nephew. Lot's family was taken into captivity due to a war that was raging against Sodom, Gomorrah, and another country. This situation shows us that we must be careful going after what our eyes tells us is plenteous and beautiful, because we could be walking into a war zone. We must seek God for His direction!

There are times in our lives that we have been distracted by the glitz and glamour of a person, place, or thing. We allow what looks good to us, to cause us to walk away from what is really good for us. Please be careful in this season not to jump into every battle, go after every highlight, or listen to every word that sounds good to you. This battle was God ordained for Abram to go help his nephew.

Every battle is not yours! Every person is not for you to rescue! Do not miss out on fulfilling your purpose because you are so busy trying to help other people find theirs. God is God for a reason! Let God be God, and you be led of Him in every situation. Abram understood that this was not a battle he could go into by himself, so God gave him 318 skilled warriors. They defeated the enemy, rescued Lot, his family, and freed others.

When God has his hand upon your life, he will use the ministry that He has given you to free others that were not even on your radar. God gave Abram strength for this journey.

Abram was recognized by the priest as a "savior," and was given many accolades. The priest even attempted to give Abram monetary rewards. Abram continued to give all honor to God, and he let them know that he would not take anything from them.

Abram shared that they could give something to the warriors, but he would not take anything. Abram stated, "I will not take anything from you, so that you may not say I made Abram rich." Abram understood that what he has, and all that is coming to his life will come from God. It is amazing that God will give you discernment on when to accept a gift, because of the type of spirit it is being given in, and the intent.

In Genesis Chapter 12, Abram was given gifts from Pharaoh and seemed to openly receive them, but chose not to accept these gifts. Why? This instance shows us that we must listen to God in every interaction, in order to know what to do in that time. We should wait for an answer from God before jumping into situations, or even accepting positions, and gifts.

James 1: 17 (GNT) says, "Every good gift and every perfect present comes from heaven; it comes down from God, the Creator of the heavenly lights, who does not change or cause darkness by turning."

Some key things to remember from this chapter:

1. We must hear from God!

2. We must learn that every gift is not a God gift!

3. Some people will just give to you to say they did something for you!

4. Be careful what you accept!

5. Abram tithed! (This shows the importance of the Tithe, the 10%)

6. Abram did not get caught up in the praise, and he brought it all back to God!

7. Be humble and God will exalt you in due time!

Prayer

Father God in the Name of Jesus, I thank you for being our Leader and our Guide in every situation in our life. Please help us listen to your voice for direction in our lives. Please let us know when to go into battle and when to be silent. God, help us know the difference when a gift is from you or not. Please help us to understand that we are nothing without you, and that you give us strength to accomplish all things. God, I thank you for leading me along this journey and I trust that you will continue to until I reach my destination. In Jesus' Name, Amen.

Chapter 4

The Vision

(Genesis Chapter 15)

God meets Abram at a moment of doubt in a vision. It is amazing that even after God has given us victory in a larger than life situation, we can still have doubt about the promise that He has given us. Abram, in the previous chapter, just went to the rescue of his nephew, and came out victorious. Always remember that if God will allow you to rescue someone else, He will always rescue you!

Abram began to ask God questions about how his heir would come. Abram had a steward in his house that was going to have a child, and he asked if this would be the child that would make him a

"Father of Many Nations". We must allow God to be God and not try to guide Him to victory! This statement means, "God does not need our help being God, but we need His help to calm down and wait." We can over think things to a point that we can become anxious and inpatient, This can cause doubt in the promise, because it seems to be late in our eyes. God told Abram look at the sky and attempt to count the stars. Abram told the Lord, he was unable to count all the stars. God let Abram know that his descendants will be many. God told Abram about the land that He will give to his descendants, and about the times that they would be in slavery for their disobedience. We serve an all-knowing and all powerful God. We must **trust** him!

> Philippians 4:6-7 "Be anxious for nothing, but in everything by prayer and supplication, with thanksgiving, let your requests be made known to God; and the peace of God, which surpasses all understanding, will guard your hearts and minds through Christ Jesus."

Questions

1. Do you have an issue with God's timing in your life?

2. Do you need to work on completely trusting God?

Prayer

Father God in the Name of Jesus, I thank for this Word. I thank you for letting me know that I am not the only one that has been inpatient on this journey to my promise. Lord please help me to wait on you and not try to figure things out on my own. Lord I need you, please guide me along this journey to my destiny. I thank you for loving me enough to put an awesome promise upon my life. Please allow me to be an example to others of your grace and mercy upon my life. In the Name of Jesus, Amen.

Chapter 5

The Decision

(Genesis Chapter 16)

One of the most difficult times on the journey to your destiny is when it begins to take longer than you initially anticipated. There are so many stories of people who have taken many detours in their lives to get to the place that God ordained for them, from the beginning of time. Our destined place is not always our comfortable place. Most times it is not! Our promised destination will usually stretch our faith, patience, determination, and even at times our mental stability. In the area of mental stability, I am not saying you are continuously losing your mind. However, I am saying that if you are not careful you can be like the man talked about in James 1:8. James 1:8 states, "A double minded man is unstable in all his ways." We must be careful along this journey to our promise to not continuously go back and forth between doubt and belief.

Abram, has been on this journey for approximately 8-9 years without a son. Abram did not begin this chapter saying anything, but his wife, Sarai, was the spokesperson. Sarai came to Abram with concern and a plan. Sarai understood that this promise had not happened, and she was concerned that it may not occur. Sarai knew that she was outside of natural child-bearing years, and she could not see the possibility of that changing. Sarai offered Abram her handmaid, Hagar, to have sex with, and that would be the child that he says God promised him.

Abram had a decision to make: 1) Listen to God and be patient. 2) Listen to my wife's plan and have a baby by Hagar. Abram had to be wrestling with some indecision and doubt regarding his promise. This seems to be true, because he did not just tell Sarai "no". Abram did not say, "I am standing on the Promise of God." Abram made the decision to go and have sexual relations with Hagar. Abram decided to help God out with his plan.

When this occurred, Abram and Hagar were able to conceive. After Sarai realized what had taken place, she became very angry. Sarai became very mean to Hagar, which caused her to run away in the wilderness. Hagar was met by an angel of the Lord and was told that her son would have a great nation. Hagar was told to go back and to name her son, Ishmael. Hagar went back and later had Ishmael.

Now Abram has a son, but this is not the son that God promised him. Abram made the decision to agree with Sarai. Abram now has to work through a dysfunctional family situation. Sarai's hatred towards Hagar has become evident, because she gave Abram a child when she could not. Abram had a decision to make, but did he make the right one?

Abram could have chosen to listen to God, but he tried to bring the promise to pass *his* way. Why didn't Abram tell Sarai, no? Why didn't Abram stand on the word from the Lord? Was he so captivated by the thought of having sex with this young woman? Was Abram doubting God? The only person who knows the truth to these questions is Abram.

The question is are we doing what Abram did in this chapter. Are we continually creating Ishmael when we have been promised another child? Stop it! Every Ishmael that you create will make it more difficult along the journey to your promise. Along your own journey, listen to God and do not let any other opinion or plan lead you away from God's plan for your life. We see a Father of the Faith go against God's perfect will for his life. Allow this to be an outline for you to do the opposite.

Prayer

Father God in the Name of Jesus, please help me listen to your voice and be consistent to its direction. God, give me the strength to stay the course when doubt comes across my mind. Lord help me!! God give me strength to say "No" when enticing alternate plans come in my path. Lord please cover me and keep me along this way! Last but not least, Father God please forgive me for all the times that I have not listened to your divine path for my life. Please forgive me for when I thought my plan was better and found out it wasn't. Please forgive me for continually being impatient with your timing and wanting it in a hurry. God please help me understand that waiting time is not wasted time! God please help me to understand that your will is perfect for my life! Thank you for always covering me and protecting me along this journey! I love you and I thank you in Jesus' name. Amen!

Chapter 6

Circumcision

(Genesis Ch. 17)

There are times in our lives that we have tried to help God! This means, "God you are taking longer than I expected and I don't think that you will mind if I take matters into my own hands." In most cases, we do not say those words, but our actions prove those are our thoughts.

We come to the place of 13 years after Ishmael was born, and God speaks to Abram. God told Abram to walk before Him. God speaks of the covenant that he will make before him and how he will be the father of many nations. God did not even mention how Abram disobeyed and adjusted the plan.

I am not sure if it because Abram immediately fell and worshipped, or if Abram had repented previously but it is not written. However, God speaks of the original covenant that must come to pass.

There are some people reading this book who have made their own adjustments to God's plan for your life. Please know that if God's promise did not die because of Abram's Ishmael, it won't die because of any Ishmael you created in your life! God changed Abram's name to Abraham which means "Father of Many". God then changed Sarai's name to Sarah which means: "Woman Minister and Noblewoman". It is amazing that even after our meddling in God's plan for our life, He will still exalt you to complete the plan He has for you. Just because you are exalted or promoted does not mean that you have done everything in the right way. The promotion that God has given may mean that his purpose for you is bigger than the mistakes that you have made. In situations like these, we must remember just because you are being "used" of God does not mean that you don't need to repent to God!

God lets Abraham know that they, he and Sarah, will have a son and Abraham laughs! God told them to name this son Isaac, which means to laugh. God told Abraham that his covenant will be with Isaac.

Abraham then asks God to have the covenant to be with Ishmael. God lets Abraham know that Ishmael will have a great nation, but the covenant will be with Isaac. Even in God's mercy Abraham still attempts to ask God to make an adjustment to his initial promise. God will stay firm to His promise, even when you are inconsistent to your commitment to his plan for your life! God gives Abraham instructions to circumcise every man and boy under his care. Circumcision is the removal of the foreskin on male genitalia. Abraham obeyed and circumcised all the men in his care, and their sons. Abraham and Ishmael were circumcised as well.

This chapter seemed to be a spiritual circumcision for Abraham as well. God was making a change in Abraham and Sarah's lives. There may be times that we feel that God is circumcising us spiritually. We may feel that God is cutting, removing, separating, and purging people, places, and things from our lives. In the midst of this circumcision, please know that it is for your betterment. God will always take care of you! God always will make the best choice for you, even if it does not cause you to feel the best.

Romans 8:28 says, "And we know that all things work together for good to them that love God, to them who are the called according to *his* purpose."

Prayer

Father God in the Name of Jesus, please forgive me for not trusting you! Please forgive me for trying to work it out myself! Please forgive me for trying to run from this time of circumcision, and not trusting you through the pain! God, help me to be faithful to you, when it doesn't feel good! God, thank you for still being there to give me another chance. God I need you, and I ask you to save me and lead me along this journey with you! I want to be right before you! God, I ask you to allow me to follow you along this road to my destiny. I thank you for loving me and protecting me! I thank you for the promise upon my life! God, please never let me forget that you have what's best for me at heart! I love you, and I thank you. In Jesus' name, Amen!

Chapter 7

Intercession

(Genesis Ch.18)

As we continue to spend time with the Lord, our relationship grows, and develops on a continuous basis. When you are cut off from society, or led to a secret place by God, it is an opportunity to see God even more. Abraham grew in God throughout his journey to the promise. As we read, Abraham doubted, made his own adjustments, and laughed at God's promise. However, God still loved him and Abraham understands what it means to repent.

In chapter 18, we see God appearing to Abraham and he is seeking God's direction. God allowed Abraham to see three men and Abraham rushed home to ask Sarah to gather good food for them. Abraham bowed before them, because he knew they were from God. The Men of God told Abraham and Sarah that Sarah would have a son, and they both began to laugh. Abraham and Sarah had an issue believing this, because Sarah was beyond child-bearing years. The Men of God asked, "Did you laugh?" Sarah denied laughing, due to the fear of what would occur.

God shared with Abraham that He is planning to destroy Sodom and Gomorrah due to their sin. The Men of God are going to orchestrate this task. Abraham began to cry out to God for the lives of those in Sodom and Gomorrah. Abraham's nephew Lot and their family lived there, and he did not want anything to happen to them. Abraham began to intercede for the people of Sodom and Gomorrah. Abraham asked God if he would destroy the city if there were 50 righteous people there. God said, "No." Abraham then asked if he would destroy the city for 45 righteous people, and God said, "No." Abraham continued to intercede for the life of those people until he came down to the number 10. Abraham asked God would he destroy the land if there were 10 righteous people in the land. God said, "No." However, there were not 10 righteous people in the land of Sodom and Gomorrah. Genesis 18:33 states, "That the Lord went his way after communing with Abraham."

Abraham has built a relationship with God that is so powerful, that he communes with God. Abraham understands how precious it is to have God reveal himself and attempted to honor the Men that God brought forth. Abraham also understands that you can ask God anything! There are times in our journey that we can keep our mouths closed when we do not understand something. We begin to try to figure things out for ourselves, and do not seek God for answers. Always remember that God loves you and cares for you! God wants to help you deal with your fears, apprehensions, problems, situations, and your destiny. We serve an omnipresent God who knows everything, but He still wants to commune with you! God wants you to talk to Him and ask Him for answers. The most important relationship in our lives, is the one that we build with God.

Questions

1. How can you build a better relationship with the Lord?

2. How much time do you spend with the Lord on a daily or weekly basis?

3. Are there times in my life that I allow the stress of life to distract me from spending time with the Lord?

Matthew 6:33 "But seek ye first the kingdom of God, and his righteousness; and all these things shall be added unto you."

Prayer

Father God in the name of Jesus, I thank you for loving me, when I have been unlovable. Please forgive me for not coming to you with all my problems and questions. Please forgive me for trying to figure things out on my own. God I surrender myself unto you and I ask you to lead me and guide me along this road to my destiny. Please God help my friends and family know you as their Lord and Savior. Please Lord help them find in you, what I found in you! Thank you for being my Savior, my God, my Shield, my Counselor, my Lawyer, my Defender, my Lead, my Guide, my Everything. Thank you for allowing me to intercede for others! Thank you for working out my situations while, I am praying for others! Lord I love you and I thank you, In Jesus' Name! Amen!

Chapter 8

Don't Lose Your Connection to God

(Genesis Chapter 19)

Lot is the nephew of Abraham and was taken by him along the journey to his promise. Abraham seemed to love Lot as a son. Abraham, in the previous chapter, has been interceding for the people of Sodom and Gomorrah. Abraham kept asking God if he would not destroy the land if there were a certain number of righteous people. Abraham got down to the number 10, and God mentioned that there were not even 10 righteous people.

Lot notices the men who had come into town, and he went out to meet them. Lot brought them into his home so that they could be protected from the men of the city, who desired to rape them. Lot went outside and spoke to the men of the city. The men of the city told Lot that they wanted the men, and they would do worse to him if he stood in their way. Lot offered the men his two virgin daughters, but the men did not want them.

The Men of God were actually Angels of the Lord. The Angels pulled Lot back into the house and let him know that they were sent by God to destroy the City. The Angels struck the men with blindness. Lot went out to his sons-in-law and told them to leave because the Lord is going to destroy the city. Lot's sons-in-law thought that he was joking. The Angels took Lot, his wife, and his two daughters with them and gave them strict instructions: don't look back, don't stay in the plain, escape to the mountains, or you will be consumed. Lot began to cry out to the Lord and was grateful that he had saved their lives. Lot asked to go into a small land, and he was allowed to go into Zoar with his children. However, Lot's wife looked back and became a pillar of salt.

Lot shows his internal connection to God in a few ways:

1. Lot puts himself in harms way to help the Angels.

2. When Lot received the Word from the Angels, he believed it and was ready to move forward.

3. Lot immediately went to tell the Word of the Lord to his sons-in-law.

4. Lot praised God for his grace and mercy for allowing him and his family the opportunity to survive.

> Proverbs 22:6 "Train up a child in the way he should go, and when he is old he will not depart from it."

The Bible speaks to the importance of a person's connections in many different instances. The Bible states that a person should love the Lord they God with all their heart, soul, mind, and strength (Matt 22:37). The Bible also talks about friendships people should have and ones they should not (Psalm 1). The Bible even discusses the type of person you should and should not marry (2 Cor.6:14-18).

In the situation of Lot's wife, she seemed to have fallen in love with some of the ways of Sodom, and she took one last look back. It is important to understand that one look back can end your life. One look back can delay the journey to your purpose. Some of us have been looking back for years, and have been stuck. We may have been stuck in regret, stuck in guilt, stuck in shame, but God wants to set you free. We as God's people, do not have any more time to waste! It is time to move forward. Do not let your past keep you stuck. Do not continue to fall in love with the wrong things and the wrong types of people! The Bible says, "Seek God while He is found and call upon him while He is near." Isaiah 55:6, KJV.

Lot was taught a love for God and it is evident in his repentant attitude in the midst of the journey out of Sodom. The story of Lot shows us that we must continue to stay connected to God, even in the midst of an ungodly environment. It is important that we teach our children the importance of having a connection with God. The same teaching we received about God, is necessary to help sustain the next generation. It is evident in the acts of Lot's daughters that they did not have the connection to God, and allowed the culture of Sodom and Gomorrah to abide inside of them. Lot's daughters got him drunk and had sex with him. The children that were born became enemy nations to the children of Israel. Any time we go outside of the will of God, we create dysfunction.

Prayer

Father God in the Name of Jesus, please allow us to keep our connection pure with you. Lord, please don't allow me to fall in love with things or people that don't align with you. Don't let me put the culture of this world above my love for you. God, help me to teach my children and those around me how to Love you even more! Please forgive me of any sins that I have committed! I love you and I thank you! In Jesus Name, Amen!

Chapter 9

Situations

(Genesis Chapter 20)

On the road to receiving the promise that God has for us, there will be different trials and situations that we will face. There may be times that we will have to come against a similar situation to see how we would handle it a second or third time. It has been said, it is better to pass the test the first time so that you do not have to repeat it. This can be the same spiritually. There may be some tests in your life that you will have to pass, in order to move forward to your promise. These tests and trials are not a punishment, they are a learning experience to help grow your faith. We can sometimes struggle with fear, doubt, anxiety, self-esteem issues, depression, sadness, anger, denial, and so many other issues. However, God will bring you out of all these issues if you allow Him. God can and will allow certain tests to come along in your life to help you understand that you are victorious! Please do not look at tests as punishment, but see them as an opportunity for your growth in God!

Abraham comes upon a familiar scenario when he and Sarah take a trip and sojourn in Gerar. Abraham told the king Abimelech that Sarah was his sister. This is not a lie, because, Sarah was his half-sister. However, Abraham did not tell the king that she was also his wife because of fear that Abimelech would kill him and take Sarah for himself. This is reminiscent of what occurred in Genesis Chapter 12, when Abraham told this to Pharaoh. It is interesting, that even after all that God has done for Abraham along the road to his destiny, fear still comes up in his life. This is also reflective of how we behave at times. We can have a moment of amnesia and forget all that God has done for us. We must know that if God be for us, He is more than the whole world against us!

God visited Abimelech in a dream and told him, that he is but a "dead man" and that Sarah is a man's wife. Abimelech obeyed God and did not touch Sarah.

Abimelech told Abraham and Sarah what God had said unto him. Abimelech was angry with them both, because he felt they lied to him. They both let him know that they are half-siblings. Abraham admitted that he told him this out of fear that he would be killed. Just as in Genesis Chapter 12, Abimelech brought riches, (sheep, oxen, men and women servants), to Abraham and gave Sarah back to him. God told Abimelech that Abraham was a prophet that would pray over him. Abraham then prayed for Abimelech, his wife, and his maidservants. After the prayer of Abraham, God healed Abimelech, his wife, and his maidservants had children. God had shut up the womb of all that were in the House of Abimelech, because of Sarah. God protected and blessed Abraham and Sarah, in the midst of their fear.

2 Timothy 1:7 says, "For God has not given us a spirit of fear, but of power and of love and of a sound mind."

Questions

1. In what areas of your life do you struggle to trust God?

2. How has fear affected your ministry?

3. Do you know when this fear started? If so, when?

4. How will you allow God to help you move past fear, so that you can do extraordinary things in Him?

Prayer

Father God in the name of Jesus, I thank you for being so merciful towards me. Please forgive me for the times that I have not trusted you. Please forgive me for the times that I allowed fear to stop me from doing your will. Help me move past fear and walk in the authority that you have given me! Deliver me so that fear can no longer hold me! Please give me Holy boldness to go forth and declare who you are! I want to walk in my destiny. I thank you Lord for having a plan for me, and I accept the plan you have for my life. I will no longer fight against your plan! I will no longer deny your plan! I will obey your will for my life! I thank you Lord for hearing me! I thank you for protecting me! I thank you Lord for freeing me! In Jesus Name, Amen!!

Chapter 10

God's Word Comes to Pass

(Genesis Chapter 21)

After years of waiting, Sarah gave birth to a son whose name is Isaac, which means "to laugh". Abraham was told by God over 20 years ago that he would be the "Father of Many Nations." Abraham and Sarah had doubts, concerns, and fears about this promise coming to pass. Now, Abraham and Sarah are staring in the face of their promised son. Sarah is very happy and talking about how unbelievable this was for her to be able to give birth at an old age.

It must have been devastating for Sarah for all these years not being able to have a child with Abraham. In a time where birthing children, especially sons, was valued tremendously, Sarah had not had a child until she was 99 years old. I could only imagine the names she may have been called, such as barren, cursed, sinner, unloved, or even unwanted. However, now she would be seen differently because God blessed her to give Abraham a son.

The couple is happy to have their promised son, but Abraham now has two sons. In a moment of interference, Abram (now Abraham) had sex with Hagar and Ishmael was born. Sarai, now Sarah, was the person that told Abraham to do it. Abraham had a choice to make at this moment back in Genesis Chapter 16. Abraham could have stood on God's promise and said "no." However, Abraham gave in to his own fleshly desire and his own doubts and laid with Hagar.

Abraham was in a moment like many of us, he could not see his promise and was scared that it really was not going to happen. Abraham doubted God! A Father of the Faith doubted God! In the midst of this doubt he created a dysfunctional situation. He did not stand on God's Word. Abraham and Sarah created a plan to help God out. Do not create an Ishmael, when you were promised an Isaac!

Sarah is now upset because Ishmael was mocking Isaac. Sarah tells Abraham to throw Hagar and Ishmael out of the camp. The person who initiated this plan for Ishmael to be born, now wants to make the evidence disappear. There are many people that want to erase their past, when they come into a new season in their life. It is important to know that your past can affect your future. Abraham is now standing in a tough situation. Abraham loves Ishmael and does not want him to leave, and Sarah does not want anything to do with him.

It is amazing what people will tolerate until they get what they really want in life. Be careful that you are not just being tolerated in someone's life. Do not settle for less!

God tells Abraham to listen to Sarah and let them go, promising that He would make Ishmael a nation because he is his seed. The promise began with Abraham but manifestation had to be carried out by God, no matter how Abraham handled the responsibility of it. Since God spoke over the life of Abraham and promised him to the Father of many nations, Abraham's son would have to have a nation. God did not say, "Your son by Sarai/Sarah would be the Father of many nations, but the promise was with Abraham's seed. You must be careful of how you spread your seed!

You cannot spread your seed any and everywhere. If you are spreading your seeds in a place or places that God did not ordain, sanctify, and approve, you are creating Ishmaels in your life that you will have to deal with later. You are creating children with Daddy issues, because they now feel abandoned. These Ishmaels in your life feel abandoned, because they were abandoned. They were displaced from a somewhat healthy environment and forced into a wilderness that they did not know. In the text, it is understood that Ishmael is of a certain age and more than likely has received training from his father on what it means to be a man and leader. However, you can never be trained on how to be abandoned and displaced from a Father who seemingly loved you at one moment, but wants nothing to do with you in the next. God was with Ishmael and he became an archer and married an Egyptian woman. God kept His promise to take care of Abraham's son, Ishmael.

Abraham later made a treaty with Abimelech after his servants had stolen some of the well water. Abraham brought Abimelech seven lambs to show that he had dug the well, and Abimelech asks

Abraham to show the same kindness to him as he had previously. After this treaty, the name of this land became Beer-sheba. Abraham then called on the name of the Lord and sojourned in the land of the Philistines. The conversation that Abraham had with God must have been epic! I wonder if he asked God, why did he have to let Ishmael leave. I wonder if he apologized for not trusting God, enough to wait on His timing for the promise. We do not know what he said when he called on the name of the Lord, but we know he did speak to God.

There are many things that we can remember from Abraham's journey to the promise, but a few have been listed below:

1. God is true to his promise! Numbers 23:19 "God is not a man, that he should lie; neither the son of man, that he should repent: hath he said, and shall he not do it? or hath he spoken, and shall he not make it good?'

2. We must trust God! Proverbs 3:5-6 says, "Trust in the LORD with all thine heart; and lean not unto thine own understanding. In all thy ways acknowledge him, and he shall direct thy paths.

3. Wait on God! Don't create an Ishmael when you were promised an Isaac! Psalm 27 :14 says, "Wait on the Lord: be of good courage, and he shall strengthen thine heart; wait, I say on the Lord."

4. God will hold you accountable. Galatians 6:7 "Be not deceived; God is not mocked: for whatsoever a man soweth, that shall he also reap."

5. God will take care of you! We serve a God that loves us beyond our mistakes, and He is willing to forgive us.

Prayer

Father God in the Name of Jesus, I thank you for giving me an opportunity to get right with you. Please save my soul. Please allow me to live for you. I believe that you are God, I believe Jesus is your Son, and that He died and rose again with all power in His hands. I thank you Lord for saving me!

Lord I ask you to help me to make the right decisions in my life. Lord, I ask you to please forgive for my wrong decisions. God please help me to be the person that you have for me to be in my life. I want to reach my promise, and don't want to create Ishmaels along the way. God I need you! Please allow me to follow the path you have created for me! I love you and I thank you In Jesus' Name, Amen!

CPSIA information can be obtained
at www.ICGtesting.com
Printed in the USA
LVHW050014061020
668044LV00012B/196